First Facts®

The Middle Ages

Kids in the Medieval World

by Sheri Johnson

Consultant:
James Masschaele
Associate Professor of Medieval History
Rutgers University
New Brunswick, New Jersey

Capstone
press®

Mankato, Minnesota

First Facts is published by Capstone Press,
151 Good Counsel Drive, P.O. Box 669, Mankato, Minnesota 56002.
www.capstonepress.com

Library of Congress Cataloging-in-Publication Data
Johnson, Sheri.
    Kids in the medieval world / by Sheri Johnson.
    p. cm. — (First facts. The Middle ages)
    Includes bibliographical references and index.
    Summary: "Describes the lives of kids during the Middle Ages, including how they
played and how they worked" — Provided by publisher.
    ISBN-13: 978-1-4296-2268-4 (hardcover)
    ISBN-10: 1-4296-2268-7 (hardcover)
    1. Children — Europe — History — Juvenile literature. 2. Social history — Medieval,
500–1500 — Juvenile literature. I. Title. II. Series.
HQ792.E8J58 2009
305.23094'0902 — dc22   2008032335

Editorial Credits

Megan Schoeneberger, editor; Kim Brown, designer; Marcie Spence, photo researcher

Photo Credits

Alamy/North Wind Picture Archives, 13; Art Resource, N.Y./The Pierpont Morgan Library, 4–5; Art Resource,
N.Y./Snark, 20; Bibliotheque de l'Ecole des Beaux-Arts, Paris, France, Giraudon/The Bridgeman Art Library
International, 12–13; Capstone Press/Karon Dubke, 21; Corbis/Gianni Dagli Orti, 9; The Granger Collection, New
York, 1, cover; Kunsthistorisches Museum, Vienna, Austria, Ali Meyer/The Bridgeman Art Library International,
14; Mary Evans Picture Library, 8, 10; Musee des Beaux-Arts, Caen, France, Giraudon/The Bridgeman Art Library
International, 18–19; Museum Narodowe, Poznan, Poland/The Bridgeman Art Library International, 16–17;
Nivaagards Malerisamling, Niva, Denmark/The Bridgeman Art Library International, 6; Private Collection, © Look
and Learn/The Bridgeman Art Library International, 11

Essential content terms are **bold** and are defined at the bottom of the page where they first appear.

1 2 3 4 5 6 14 13 12 11 10 09

Table of Contents

Get to Work!

Imagine you are just 7 years old. You have to work all day. It sounds horrible, but this was normal life for kids in medieval times.

In Europe during the Middle Ages, childhood was short. By age 13, childhood was over. Kids were then thought of as adults.

Kids in the Middle Ages

Europe
476 ~ 1500

Medieval Fact!

In the Middle Ages, kids wore loose-fitting clothing. Fashions were similar across Europe.

Rich and Poor

In the Middle Ages, **nobles** had a lot of money and land. They lived in castles or big houses called manors.

But most families and children were poor. These **peasants** farmed land owned by nobles. They lived in wooden homes with straw roofs. The homes had only one room. The family used the room for cooking, eating, and sleeping. At night, farm animals often slept in the room too.

noble — a person born of high rank or wealth
peasant — a poor farmer

Baby Days

In the Middle Ages, life was hard from the start. Babies were born at home without doctors. Some died at birth. By age 5, one out of four children had died.

Many parents worried that their children's bodies would grow crooked. They wrapped babies tightly with cloth. Parents thought this would help kids grow straight and tall.

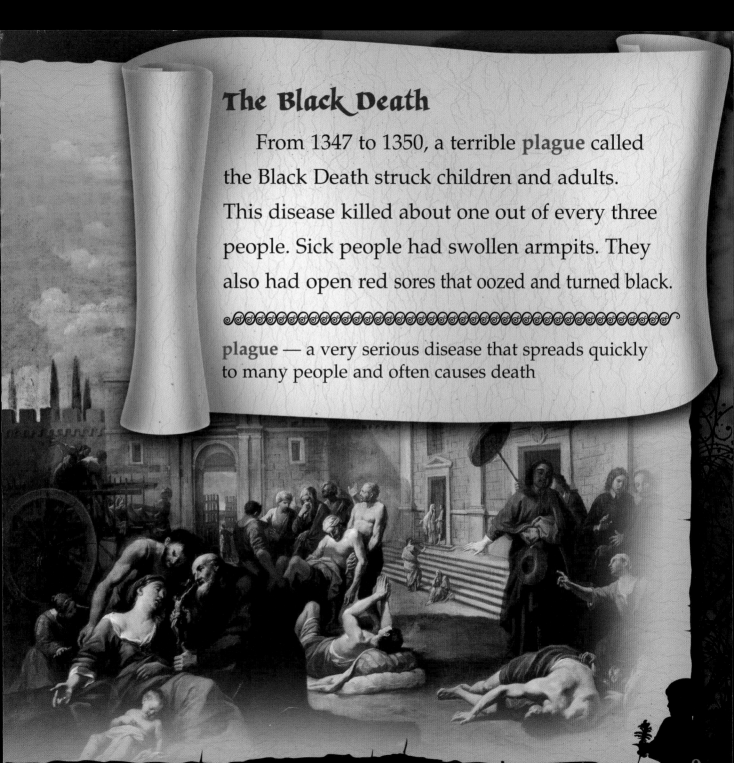

The Black Death

From 1347 to 1350, a terrible **plague** called the Black Death struck children and adults. This disease killed about one out of every three people. Sick people had swollen armpits. They also had open red sores that oozed and turned black.

plague — a very serious disease that spreads quickly to many people and often causes death

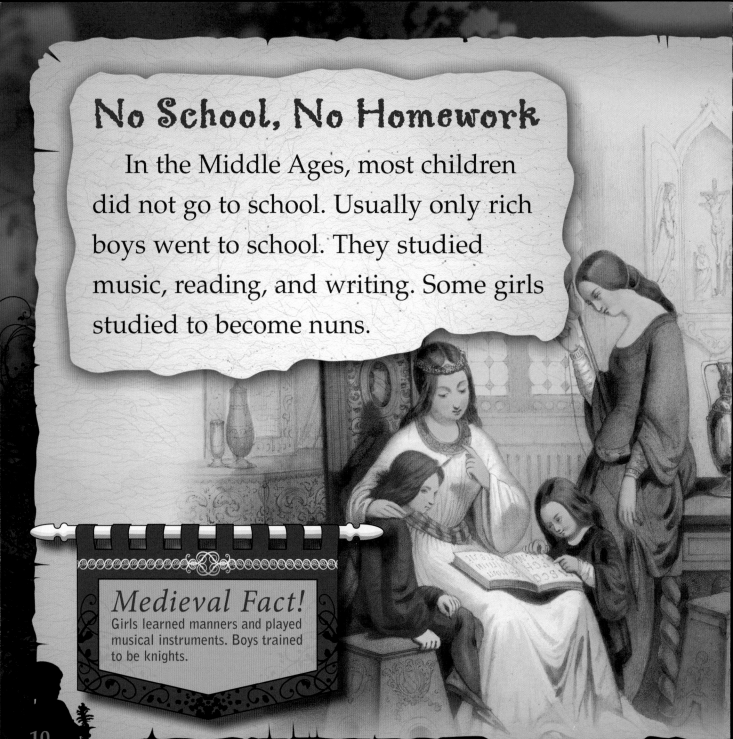

No School, No Homework

In the Middle Ages, most children did not go to school. Usually only rich boys went to school. They studied music, reading, and writing. Some girls studied to become nuns.

Medieval Fact!
Girls learned manners and played musical instruments. Boys trained to be knights.

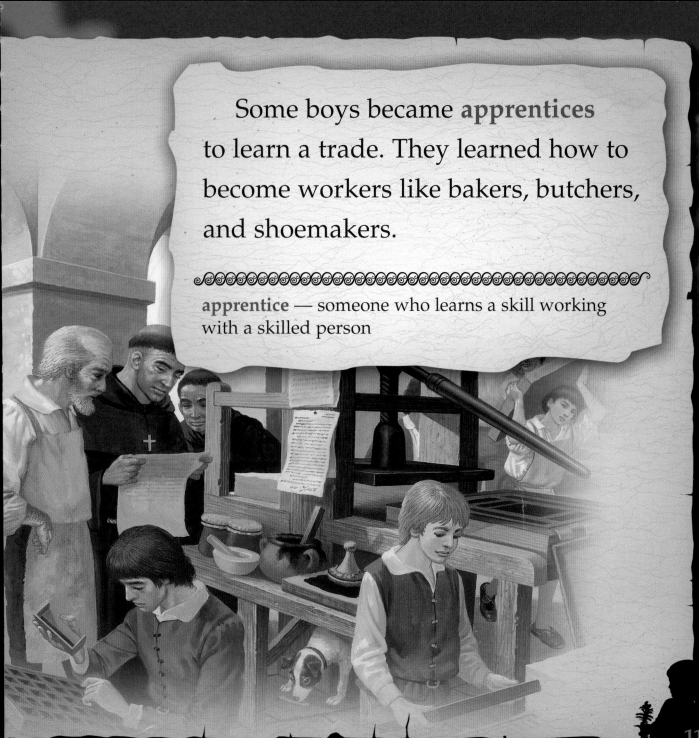

Some boys became **apprentices** to learn a trade. They learned how to become workers like bakers, butchers, and shoemakers.

apprentice — someone who learns a skill working with a skilled person

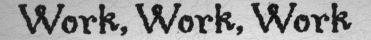

Work, Work, Work

Peasant kids didn't have the time or money to go to school. Their parents needed their help at home.

Girls and boys had different jobs. Girls sewed, cleaned, and cooked. They also looked after younger brothers and sisters. Boys helped farm. Younger boys cleared stones from fields and scared away birds. Older boys herded animals.

Medieval Fact!

Most people in the Middle Ages could not read or write.

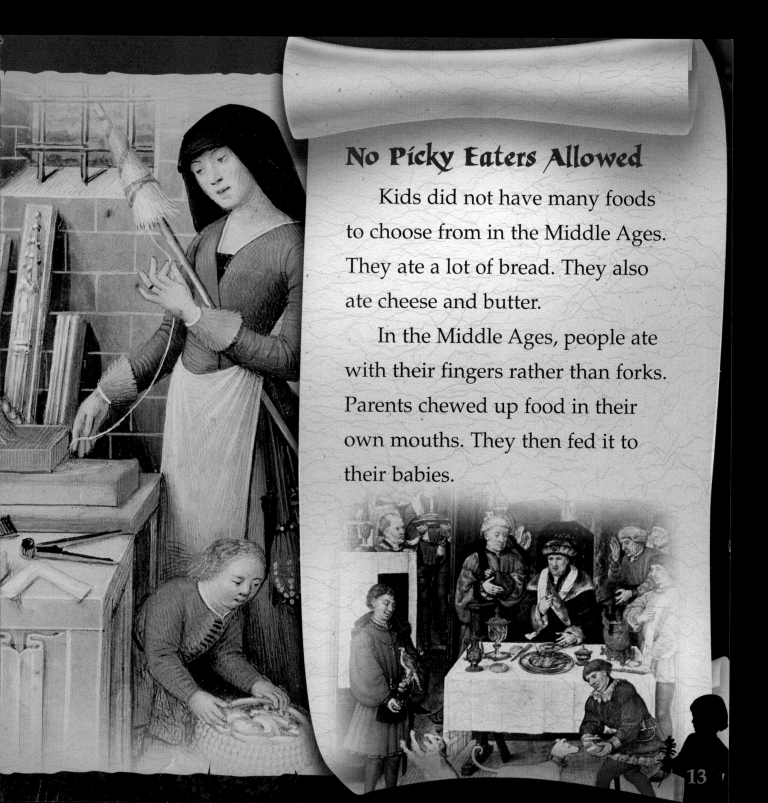

No Picky Eaters Allowed

Kids did not have many foods to choose from in the Middle Ages. They ate a lot of bread. They also ate cheese and butter.

In the Middle Ages, people ate with their fingers rather than forks. Parents chewed up food in their own mouths. They then fed it to their babies.

Time for Toys

Medieval kids worked hard, but they also found time to play. Young children played with balls, hoops, kites, tops, marbles, and **stilts**. Girls played with dolls made from rags, baked clay, or wood. Boys played with bows and arrows.

stilt — a pole that has a rest or strap for the foot to make the person taller by standing on it

Fun and Games

Children and adults enjoyed dancing and music. They also played games such as **chess**. Kids enjoyed wrestling, playing tag, running in foot races, and playing ball games. Young boys played war games. These games prepared them to become knights.

chess — a board game for two people with 16 pieces each

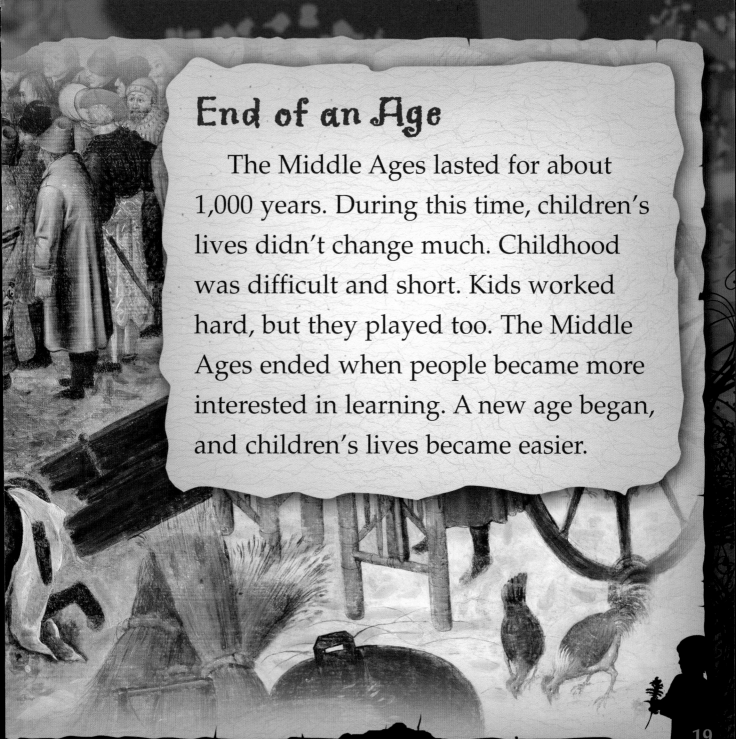

End of an Age

The Middle Ages lasted for about 1,000 years. During this time, children's lives didn't change much. Childhood was difficult and short. Kids worked hard, but they played too. The Middle Ages ended when people became more interested in learning. A new age began, and children's lives became easier.

Amazing but True!

When medieval kids got sick, parents cared for them with homemade medicine. Children only saw doctors if they were really sick. Sometimes doctors would taste a patient's pee to find out what was wrong!

Try It Out: Spinning Top

Medieval children used to play with tops. You can create your own modern day top. Watch the colors on the top when you spin it on a flat surface. Just try to avoid getting pencil all over!

What You Need

- a pencil
- markers, colored pencils, or crayons
- cardboard
- scissors
- tape

What You Do

1. Trace a circle about 3 inches (8 centimeters) in diameter on the cardboard.
2. Carefully cut out your circle.
3. Use your markers, colored pencils, or crayons to draw a spiral line from the center of the cardboard around and around to the outside edge. If you want, add more colored lines.
4. Poke the pencil through the center of the circle so the point sticks through. Keep the cardboard near the bottom of the pencil.
5. If the cardboard won't stay put, tape it in place.
6. Spin the top on a hard flat surface.

Glossary

apprentice (uh-PREN-tiss) — someone who learns a trade by working with a skilled person

chess (CHESS) — a board game for two people played on a checkerboard

noble (NOH-buhl) — a person of high rank or birth

peasant (PEZ-uhnt) — a poor farmer

plague (PLAYG) — a very serious disease that spreads quickly to many people and often causes death

stilt (STILT) — a pole, with a rest or strap for the foot, used on each foot to raise the wearer above the ground in walking

Read More

Benduhn, Tea. *The Middle Ages.* Life Long Ago.
Milwaukee: Weekly Reader Early Learning Library, 2006.

Elliott, Lynne. *Children and Games in the Middle Ages.*
Medieval World. New York: Crabtree, 2004.

Hodge, Susie. *Medieval Europe.* Historic Civilizations.
Milwaukee: Gareth Stevens, 2005.

Shuter, Jane. *The Middle Ages.* History Opens Windows.
Chicago: Heinemann, 2007.

Internet Sites

FactHound offers a safe, fun way to find
educator-approved Internet sites related to this book.

Here's what you do:
    1. Visit *www.facthound.com*
    2. Choose your grade level.
    3. Begin your search.

This book's ID number is 9781429622684.

FactHound will fetch the best sites for you!

Index